THIS
BOOK
BELONGS
TO...

_1885_

Name: Age:

Favourite player:

2023/24

My Predictions   Actual

The Lions' final position:

The Lions' top scorer:

Championship winners:

Championship top scorer:

FA Cup winners:

Contributors: Peter Rogers

A TWOCAN PUBLICATION

©2023. Published by twocan under licence from Millwall Football Club.

Every effort has been made to ensure the accuracy of information within this publication but the publishers cannot be held responsible for any errors or omissions. Views expressed are those of the authors and do not necessarily represent those of the publishers or the football club. All rights reserved.

978-1-915571-65-6

PICTURE CREDITS: Alamy, Millwall FC, Reuters.

22

errea

CONTENTS

THE CHAMPIONSHIP
SQUAD
2023/24

Danny McNAMARA **2**

POSITION: Defender **COUNTRY:** Republic of Ireland **DOB:** 27/12/1998

After successful loan spells with The Exiles and at Scottish Premier League side St Johnstone, McNamara made his first-team debut in an Emirates FA Cup Third Round tie at Boreham Wood in January 2021. After seven further appearances, an assured and confident McNamara was rewarded with a new long-term contract.

The 2021/22 campaign saw McNamara firmly establish himself in Gary Rowett's XI, scoring his first two senior goals on his 50th appearance against Barnsley and winning two end-of-season awards - the Junior Lions Player of the Season and second place in the Millwall Supporters' Club Player of the Season vote.

The defender - who occupies the number two shirt - is the club's first-choice right-back and a fans' favourite, making his 100th appearance at Middlesbrough on the opening day of the 2023/24 campaign.

Murray
WALLACE

3

POSITION: Defender **COUNTRY:** Scotland **DOB:** 10/01/1993

Defender Murray Wallace joined Millwall on a free transfer from Scunthorpe United in June 2018. The defender's commitment and athleticism have made him a popular figure at The Den albeit before suffering a nasty injury at Hull City in February 2019, but his standout moments have undoubtedly come in the Emirates FA Cup.

Millwall's run to the Quarter-Finals of the 2018/19 competition - becoming the last non-Premier League side remaining - witnessed two vital winning goals from Murray against Everton and AFC Wimbledon, the former coming in an iconic final minute at The Den back in late January.

The left-back experienced a solid season in The Lions' defence in 2019/20, making 47 appearances, in which he was converted to playing in a wing-back role by boss Gary Rowett.

The Scot signed a new long-term contract at The Den in February 2021 and has continued as a mainstay in Rowett's defence, earning the 2021/22 Millwall Supporters' Club Player of the Season crown following an outstanding campaign. Wallace made 39 appearances in all competitions in 2022/23.

Shaun
HUTCHINSON

4

POSITION: Defender   **COUNTRY:** England   **DOB:** 23/11/1990

Shaun Hutchinson joined Millwall in 2016 after his contract with Fulham came to an end. He appeared in all 46 Sky Bet Championship games for The Lions in 2017/18, scoring twice. He and James Meredith were the only players to achieve the feat of appearing in every league match during the campaign.

Following into the 2018/19 term, Shaun suffered with occasional injuries, making 26 appearances and scoring one goal - also regularly captaining the side in the early months of the season.

The defender's goal return was improved in 2019/20, as Hutchinson scored six times in 38 appearances, including a vital winner in a rain-soaked 1-0 victory at Preston North End.

Hutchinson missed part of 2021/22 through injury, but still managed to make 32 appearances in a side which just missed out on a place in the Championship Play-Offs, before going on to play 30 times in 2022/23.

THE CHAMPIONSHIP
SQUAD
2023/24

Jake COOPER 5

POSITION: Defender **COUNTRY:** England **DOB:** 03/02/1995

The defender initially joined the club on loan from Reading in January 2017, but after impressing and helping The Lions on the way to the Sky Bet League One Play-Off Final trophy, Millwall boss Neil Harris opted to bring Jake to the club permanently that summer.

After playing every minute of a second successive season in 2019/20, an incredible run for the defender came to an end in December 2020 as he missed his first game in 136 matches away to Blackburn Rovers, after suffering a dislocated shoulder during a trip to Birmingham City - remarkably, Cooper played on until the end of the game!

After 46 appearances in 2020/21, the defender appeared a further 46 times in 2021/22, scoring four times - and racking up an incredible feat of every single goal being a matchwinner!

The season of 2022/23 saw Cooper make his 300th appearance for Millwall - and the defender will hope to build on that over the course of 2023/24.

Kevin NISBET 7

POSITION: Striker **COUNTRY:** Scotland **DOB:** 08/03/1997

Millwall announced the signing of Kevin Nisbet from Hibernian on 10th June 2023. Nisbet has spent his career to date in Scotland, playing for the likes of Partick Thistle, Dumbarton, Raith Rovers and Dunfermline Athletic, before a move to Easter Road in 2020 saw the frontman become one of the hottest prospects north of the border.

With 19 goals to his name in 2020/21, Nisbet was included in the Scotland squad travelling to the delayed EURO 2020, playing a part in all three games - including the Wembley showdown against England - from the bench.

Europa Conference League experience followed for the attacker, with 21 goals in his last two seasons earning Nisbet a move to South London. The Scot scored for fun in pre-season and made his Lions debut at the Riverside Stadium.

THE CHAMPIONSHIP SQUAD 2023/24

Billy MITCHELL
8

POSITION: Midfielder **COUNTRY:** England **DOB:** 07/04/2001

Local lad Billy Mitchell has progressed through the ranks at Millwall over a number of years and has recently enjoyed a fruitful season with the club's Under 18 and Under 23 sides.

Billy's displays since saw him rewarded with his first professional contract at the club, and his first-team debut in The Lions' final game of the 2018/19 League season at Wigan Athletic, playing 12 minutes and receiving a rapturous reception from the travelling fans as he made his bow.

Mitchell's rise continued in 2019/20, as he claimed the Young Player of the Year crown, before the midfielder scored his first senior Lions goal in a 4-1 win over Bristol City in the final home game of the 2020/21 campaign.

The midfielder then nailed down a first-team berth in 2021/22, playing 45 times in the heart of Gary Rowett's midfield, before going on to make 36 Championship appearances in 2022/23.

Tom
BRADSHAW
9

POSITION: Striker   COUNTRY: Wales   DOB: 27/07/1992

Tom Bradshaw arrived at The Den in August 2018 on an initial loan deal from Barnsley, becoming a permanent club-record in January 2019.

Tom's start to his Millwall career came with 10 Championship appearances, before unfortunately being struck down with a long-term knee ligament injury, which ruled him out for the rest of his debut campaign.

The striker did recover, however, and is a part of Gary Rowett's plans, appearing regularly in the matchday squad. Bradshaw scored nine times in 2021/22, including in five consecutive games, to earn himself a new contract. Bradshaw enjoyed a fruitful campaign in 2022/23, finding the net 17 times.

Zian
FLEMMING

10

POSITION: Midfielder   **COUNTRY:** Netherlands   **DOB:** 01/08/1998

Zian Flemming signed a long-term contract at Millwall on 24th June 2022, putting pen-to-paper after joining from Eredivisie side Fortuna Sittard for an undisclosed fee.

Flemming, who hails from Amsterdam, began his career in the Netherlands in the Ajax youth system before moving on to PEC Zwolle, where he made 29 Eredivisie appearances before sealing a move to Sittard in August 2020.

The Dutchman then flourished with Fortuna, scoring 12 goals in two consecutive seasons, including strikes against giants Feyenoord, and five goals in his last four matches of the campaign.

The signing of Zian proved to be a pivotal one for Gary Rowett, as he scored 15 goals in 44 Championship appearances, propelling The Lions to the cusp of the Play-Offs.

THE CHAMPIONSHIP
SQUAD
2023/24

Ryan LONGMAN **11**

POSITION: Midfielder   **COUNTRY: England**   **DOB: 06/11/2000**

Millwall Football Club announced the signing of Ryan Longman on a season-long loan from Hull City on Friday 1 September 2023. The 22-year-old attacker, who can play in a number of positions, became Gary Rowett's seventh signing of the summer transfer window.

Longman, originally from Redhill in Surrey, began his professional career at Brighton & Hove Albion and made his debut in the 2019/20 season as The Seagulls took on Aston Villa in a Carabao Cup tie.

The Hull City man then joined AFC Wimbledon on loan for the 2020/21 campaign, scoring nine times in all competitions, including two in a London derby against Charlton Athletic. Originally joining The Tigers on loan before completing a permanent move, Longman added 36 appearances and five more goals to his name across 2021/22, with a further full season at the MKM Stadium taking place in 2022/23.

Allan CAMPBELL **14**

POSITION: Midfielder   **COUNTRY: Scotland**   **DOB: 04/07/1998**

Millwall Football Club announced the signing of Allan Campbell on a season-long loan from Luton Town on Friday 1 September 2023. The 25-year-old midfielder became Gary Rowett's eighth signing of the summer transfer window and was the second to join on deadline day.

The Scot's career began at Motherwell, where he scored on his third professional appearance, going on to make 160 appearances across seven years north of the border.

With Europa League experience to his name, Campbell then moved south to Luton Town in the summer of 2021, making almost 90 appearances across two seasons in all competitions as The Hatters competed in back-to-back Play-Off campaigns in the second tier, eventually winning promotion to the Premier League in the latter.

Joe
BRYAN
15

POSITION: Defender   **COUNTRY:** England   **DOB:** 17/09/1993

Millwall Football Club announced the signing of Joe Bryan on 30th June 2023. The 29-year-old free agent joined the club on a long-term deal with the left-back becoming Gary Rowett's second signing of the summer transfer window.

Counting Bristol City, Fulham and OGC Nice among his former clubs, Bryan made his competitive debut on the opening day of 2023/24 at Middlesbrough.

THE CHAMPIONSHIP
SQUAD
2023/24

Ryan
LEONARD
18

POSITION: Midfielder   **COUNTRY:** England   **DOB:** 24/05/1992

Ryan Leonard initially joined Millwall on loan until January 2019, where he has since completed a club-record undisclosed fee move to The Lions from Sheffield United.

The midfielder signed for The Blades for a undisclosed fee in January 2018, but was captured by Harris and Millwall on Deadline Day in August 2018. Ryan had been a regular in the middle of the park under Harris, making 37 League appearances and scoring on two occasions. In 2019/20, Leonard scored a Goal of the Season contender in a 1-0 victory at struggling Hull City.

However, Leonard has shown his versatility and ability to operate wherever asked under Gary Rowett, having excelled at right-back, right-wing-back, attacking midfield and centre-back in addition to his usual position.

The utility man frustratingly found his opportunities limited due to injury in 2021/22, but Leonard's popularity rose in 21 appearances for Gary Rowett's side, as well as 18 times in 2023/24.

Duncan
WATMORE
19

POSITION: Striker   **COUNTRY:** England   **DOB:** 08/03/1994

Duncan Watmore signed for Millwall from Middlesbrough for an undisclosed fee on 31st January 2023.

The Cheshire-born forward, who can play across the front-line, scored three goals for The Lions in 2022/23, including two on the final day at home to Blackburn Rovers.

Matija ŠARKIĆ

20

POSITION: **Goalkeeper** COUNTRY: **Montenegro** DOB: **23/07/1997**

Millwall Football Club announced the signing of Matija Šarkić from Wolverhampton Wanderers on 3rd August 2023.

The 26-year-old goalkeeper joined the club on a long-term contract for an undisclosed fee and became number five in the door for Gary Rowett during the summer transfer window.

THE CHAMPIONSHIP
SQUAD
2023/24

Aidomo
EMAKHU

22

POSITION: Striker **COUNTRY:** Republic of Ireland **DOB:** 26/10/2003

Aidomo Emakhu joined The Lions from Shamrock Rovers on 1st January 2023.

He made one Sky Bet Championship appearance - from the bench - against Burnley in 2022/23 and started the new season by assisting Romain Esse for his first-ever professional goal at Middlesbrough on 5th August.

George
SAVILLE

23

POSITION: Midfielder **COUNTRY:** Northern Ireland **DOB:** 01/06/1993

George Saville returned to Millwall Football Club for an undisclosed fee on a long-term contract in July 2021.

In The Lions' first season back at Sky Bet Championship level after winning the League One Play-Offs, Saville hit the back of the net 10 times in a campaign which saw the midfielder play 50 times, earning international recognition with Northern Ireland in the process.

A multi-million pound move to Middlesbrough arose in August 2018, but after three years away, Saville returned to The Den as Gary Rowett's fifth signing of the 2021 summer window.

In his first season back in SE16, Saville made 40 appearances and scored three times, with all his strikes coming at The Den. The 2022/23 season was an arduous one for the midfielder as he played 53 times for club and country, scoring twice.

THE CHAMPIONSHIP SQUAD
2023/24

Casper DE NORRE — 24

POSITION: **Midfielder**   COUNTRY: **Belgium**   DOB: **07/02/1997**

Millwall Football Club announced the signing of Casper De Norre from OH Leuven on 21st July 2023. The 26-year-old midfielder joined on a long-term contract for an undisclosed fee and became The Lions' fourth signing of the summer transfer window.

The Belgian, who can play in central midfield or at right-back, made his professional debut for Belgian Division One side St. Truiden, where he spent three-and-a-half more years before opting for a short hop to Genk, where he gained Belgian Under 21 experience and tasted Champions League football against the likes of Liverpool and Napoli.

A move to Leuven then materialised in October 2020, with De Norre part of the OH side who racked up consecutive mid-table finishes in the Jupiler League. Casper made his Millwall debut at Middlesbrough on the opening day of the 2023/24 campaign.

Connal TRUEMAN — 27

POSITION: **Goalkeeper**   COUNTRY: **England**   DOB: **26/03/1996**

Connal Trueman bolsters The Lions' goalkeeping options. The 26-year-old joined The Lions following eight years at his home town club, Birmingham City, where he made 14 appearances for The Blues.

The young goalkeeper also had several loan spells away from club with his two most recent at Swindon Town and Oxford United and joined the ranks in SE16 looking to add competition to Matija Šarkić and Bartosz Białkowski.

Romain **ESSE**

25

POSITION: Midfielder **COUNTRY:** England **DOB:** 13/05/2005

Raising through the ranks at The Den, Romain Esse made his Sky Bet Championship debut in a 2-0 win over Watford on Boxing Day after appearing in a friendly match against Brondby IF.

A regular in The Lions' Under 18 and Under 21s set-ups, the midfielder appeared in SE16 for the first time in Millwall's 3-0 success over Rotherham United on New Year's Day 2023.

From there, Esse has excited many and found the back of the net for the very first time during Millwall's 1-0 win at Middlesbrough to kick-off the 2023/24 season.

Bartosz
BIAŁKOWSKI 33

POSITION: Goalkeeper   COUNTRY: Poland   DOB: 06/07/1987

Polish international Bartosz Białkowski originally signed a season-long loan deal at Millwall for the 2019/20 campaign from Ipswich Town, in late July 2019.

Białkowski made his move to The Den a permanent one in January 2020, going on to win the Millwall Supporters' Club 2019/20 Player of the Year crown and sharing the Sky Bet Championship Golden Glove - for amassing 16 clean sheets - with Brentford stopper David Raya.

The Pole continued his fine form into the 2020/21 campaign, becoming a back-to-back Player of the Year winner, and further rubber-stamped his credentials in 2021/22 with a top three finish for the third consecutive season.

Białkowski continues to challenge for the number one spot in SE16 as he moves into a fifth season at the club.

THE CHAMPIONSHIP
SQUAD
2023/24

George
HONEYMAN **39**

POSITION: Midfielder   COUNTRY: England   DOB: 08/09/1994

George Honeyman joined The Lions on a long-term contract for an undisclosed fee on 28th June 2022.

The attacking midfielder began his career at Sunderland, where he spent five seasons, including gaining Premier League experience, before moving on to Hull City in 2019.

A main part of the side which won the Sky Bet League One title in 2020/21 - alongside George Long - Honeyman impressed in a creative role for The Tigers, before making 36 Championship appearances and scoring five goals last season.

Honeyman made 40 appearances for Millwall during his first season at the club, scoring once, against Coventry City at The Den in August 2022.

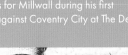

Wes
HARDING **45**

POSITION: Defender   COUNTRY: Jamaica   DOB: 26/10/1996

Millwall Football Club announced the signing of Wes Harding on 21st July 2023. The 26-year-old free agent became The Lions' third signing of the summer transfer window and bolsters Gary Rowett's squad ahead of the 2023/24 season.

The versatile defender - who can play anywhere across the back line - most recently played for Rotherham United and arrives in SE16 on the back of three years with The Millers.

A product of Birmingham City's youth system, the Jamaican made 60 appearances for The Blues before making the move to Yorkshire in August 2020.

In his time with Rotherham, Harding was a vital member of the side which won promotion from League One in 2021/22, making 47 appearances in all competitions as they finished in second place.

21

ONE OF THE HARDEST THINGS TO DO IN FOOTBALL IS TO STICK THE BALL IN THE BACK OF THE NET.

NOT LEAST BECAUSE THERE ARE USUALLY ELEVEN OTHER PLAYERS TRYING TO STOP YOU DOING JUST THAT!

SHOOTING
FROM DISTANCE

Good service is obviously important, and a good understanding with your striking partner is also vital, but when it comes to spectacular strikes, practice is the key to hitting a consistently accurate and powerful shot and to developing the timing and power required.

EXERCISE

A small-sided pitch is set up with two 18-yard boxes put together, but the corners of the pitch are cut off as shown in the diagram. There are five players per team, including goalkeepers, but only one player is allowed in the opponent's half.

The aim of the drill is to work a shooting opportunity when you have the ball, with the likely chance being to shoot from outside your opponent's penalty area, from distance. The teams take it in turns to release the ball into play from their own 'keeper - usually by rolling out to an unmarked player.

18 YDS

KEY FACTORS

1. Attitude to shooting - be positive, have a go!
2. Technique - use laces, hit through the ball.
3. Do not sacrifice accuracy for power.
4. Wide angle shooting - aim for the far post.
5. Always follow up for rebounds!

The size of the pitch can be reduced for younger players, and it should be noted that these junior players should also be practicing with a size 4 or even a size 3 ball, depending on their age.

SOCCER
SKILLS

KEVIN
NISBET
7

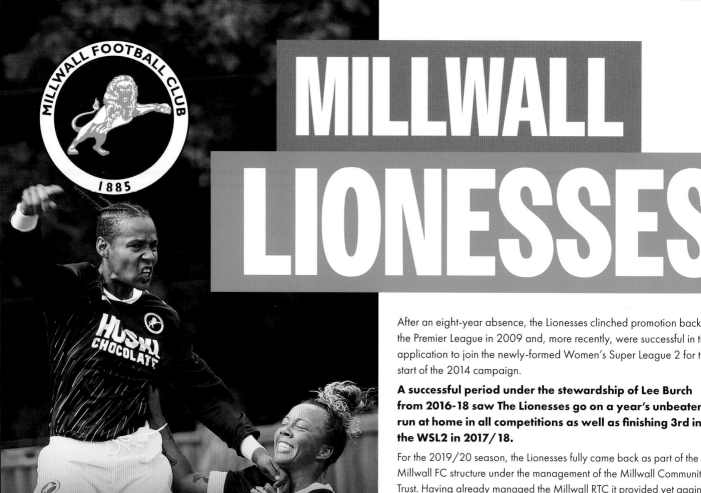

MILLWALL LIONESSES

After an eight-year absence, the Lionesses clinched promotion back to the Premier League in 2009 and, more recently, were successful in their application to join the newly-formed Women's Super League 2 for the start of the 2014 campaign.

A successful period under the stewardship of Lee Burch from 2016-18 saw The Lionesses go on a year's unbeaten run at home in all competitions as well as finishing 3rd in the WSL2 in 2017/18.

For the 2019/20 season, the Lionesses fully came back as part of the Millwall FC structure under the management of the Millwall Community Trust. Having already managed the Millwall RTC it provided yet again a full pathway for young female footballers to continue their development.

The Lionesses are currently playing in the London & South East Regional Women's League, alongside local rivals such as: Fulham, Dulwich Hamlet & Dartford. All Millwall Lionesses home games for the 2023/24 campaign are to be played at the St Paul's Sports Ground in Rotherhithe.

The Lionesses started the 2023/24 campaign in good form with a 2-2 opening-day draw at Sutton United followed by a 3-1 victory over Dorking Wanderers with goals from Shannan Drewe and two from Emma Whitter.

One of the oldest clubs and most recognisable names in women's football, Millwall Lionesses Football Club is fiercely proud of its richly deserved reputation as a pioneering force of the British Women's game.

First founded in 1972, The Lionesses became the first club in the country to be officially affiliated to a professional men's team in the 1980s, as Millwall FC sought to strengthen their ties with the local community.

With the support of the Millwall Community programme, The Lionesses quickly became a leading light in women's football. They were the first club in the country to open a Girls Centre of Excellence, allowing them to develop talented players from the age of eight, right through to senior level.

Many graduates of The Lionesses' youth system have gone on to win honours, both on an international and domestic stage, including such legends of the women's game as Hope Powell, Pauline Cope, Mary Phillip and Katie Chapman.

Founder members of the Women's Premier League in 1991, the club also collected its first major silverware that season, as Yvonne Baldeo netted the only goal of the game to defeat Doncaster Belles in the Women's FA Cup.

The Lionesses repeated that feat six years later, with Lou Waller's winner securing a 1-0 victory over Wembley in the final at Upton Park. Millwall collected a domestic cup double that season, beating Everton 2-1 at Underhill to lift the Women's Premier League Cup for the first time.

THE LIONESSES CELEBRATE WINNING THE 1997 WOMENS FA CUP

DAZZLING
DEFENDERS

BARRY KITCHENER, KEITH STEVENS AND PAUL ROBINSON WERE ALL OUTSTANDING LIONS DEFENDERS. CONTINUING THAT TRADITION IS MILLWALL MAINSTAY JAKE COOPER.

Second in the all-time appearances table for Millwall Football Club, Keith Stevens was a firm fan favourite as a player and manager over two decades at The Den.

A regular at the old and new versions of the stadiums, Stevens was a product of The Lions' youth system before going on to play over 550 times in a blue shirt.

'Rhino' then had a stint as manager alongside Alan McLeary, with the pair steering a young Millwall side to the Auto Windscreen Shield Final against Wigan Athletic in 1999.

To a certain generation of Millwall fan, there is no greater player than Barry Kitchener.

The man with the most appearances in the history of Millwall Football Club started his journey with The Lions in 1966, mainly playing in Division Two before exiting South London in 1982.

The man who also had a spell as caretaker manager in 1982, Kitchener is widely regarded as one of The Lions' landmark players since the club's inception in 1885.

BARRY KITCHENER

DATE OF BIRTH:	11 December 1947
PLACE OF BIRTH:	Dagenham
NATIONALITY:	English
LIONS APPEARANCES:	596
LIONS GOALS:	28
LIONS DEBUT:	11 February 1967

Birmingham City 2-0 Millwall (Division Two)

KEITH STEVENS

DATE OF BIRTH:	21 June 1964
PLACE OF BIRTH:	Merton
NATIONALITY:	English
LIONS APPEARANCES:	557
LIONS GOALS:	10
LIONS DEBUT:	29 April 1981

Oxford United 1-0 Millwall (Division Three)

Lions legend, Paul Robinson has done it all at Millwall Football Club.

Making 361 appearances over twelve seasons in South London - and scoring 23 goals - the man affectionately known as 'Robbo' most famously captained the Lions to a 2010 Sky Bet League One Play-Off Final victory over Swindon Town at Wembley Stadium.

The defender typified the Millwall spirit during his playing days, putting his body on the line and shedding blood, sweat and tears in his commitment to the cause.

PAUL ROBINSON

DATE OF BIRTH: 7 January 1982

PLACE OF BIRTH: Barnet

NATIONALITY: English

LIONS APPEARANCES: 361

LIONS GOALS: 23

LIONS DEBUT: 9 November 2002
Millwall 2-1 Preston North End (Division One)

JAKE COOPER

DATE OF BIRTH: 3 February 1995

PLACE OF BIRTH: Ascot

NATIONALITY: English

LIONS APPEARANCES: 300*

LIONS GOALS: 24*

LIONS DEBUT: 21 January 2017
Bradford City 1-1 Millwall (League One)

*AS AT THE END OF THE 2022/23 SEASON

'Coops' made his 300th Millwall appearance on the final day of the 2022/23 Sky Bet Championship season against Blackburn Rovers.

A mainstay of The Lions' defence and into his eighth season at the club, the towering centre-back has been a part of some of Millwall's most memorable moments, including last-minute winners at Sheffield United - continuing his love of scoring against The Blades!

Making the number five shirt his own, supporters will hope to see Jake carry on his career at The Den for many years to come.

AIDOMO
EMAKHU

22

FOOTY
PHRASES

...BUT CAN YOU WORK OUT WHICH ONE?

```
C A E S W Y V Y B H U G N U R Y M M U D
V U Q I D E R B Y D A Y O L U R T S S U
K F A D J L G T X T F C B E I A K C F P
I B H E O T L P Z R V N M W O J I R Y A
C M O F F S I D E R U L E E D S P E Y H
M E R U E I J R D E D A Q G S H L A X C
R X E R N H A T T R I C K O I L A M R T
E I Y O W W S L S N O W R S O Z Y E Y A
D C A A Z L W S J K T K Y V K B M R T M
A A L P X A U Y H M I D F I E D A R O E
E N P T K N F W G C P L J K A M K N L H
H W E J A I L O K H A O F O H I E C G T
G A M E O F T W O H A L V E S T R N U F
N V A I A H E S L F J D U A O I U O T O
I E G B I C L A S S A C T U P F G E V N
V D G O A E E U C K S S C Y W U L Q L A
I R I R Q G M N S A C H G H D O S F G M
D V B A C K O F T H E N E T Z P X B N A
```

Back of the Net	**Diving Header**	**Half Volley**	**Offside Rule**
Big Game Player	**Dugout**	**Hat-trick**	**One-touch**
Brace	**Dummy Run**	**Keepie Uppie**	**Playmaker**
Class Act	**Final Whistle**	**Man of the Match**	**Scissor Kick**
Derby Day	**Game of Two Halves**	**Mexican Wave**	**Screamer**

PLAYER
OF THE SEASON

Zian Flemming won Millwall Football Club's 2022/23 Player of the Year trophy.

The Dutchman midfielder enjoyed a fruitful and influential campaign during his first season in South London, scoring 15 times and providing numerous assists as The Lions went close to the Sky Bet Championship Play-Offs.

Donning the number 10 shirt, Flemming quickly had a chant dedicated to his place of birth, Amsterdam, and his dislike for local rivals West Ham United, and also netted the club's Goal of the Season award for his strike at Rotherham United.

One of - if not the - first names on Gary Rowett's teamsheet, Zian excited with his skill, flair and keen eye for goal, making 44 appearances across the season since moving from Fortuna Sittard in the summer of 2022.

YOUNG PLAYER OF THE SEASON

Millwall Football Club's 2022/23 Young Player of the Year trophy was won by Romain Esse.

At just 18-years-old, the young attacker has already made his mark in SE16 and has a bright future ahead of him. Esse impressed in the club's youth set-up enough to earn him a place on the substitute's bench for the Boxing Day trip to Watford, in which he came on and almost added a late third in The Lions' 2-0 win at Vicarage Road.

From there, Romain has gone from strength to strength and scored his first professional goal in the 2023/24 opening day win at Middlesbrough.

ROMAIN ESSE

ZIAN FLEMMING

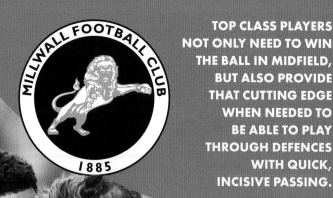

THE WALL PASS

With teams being very organised in modern football, it can be very difficult to break them down and create scoring opportunities. One of the best ways to achieve this is by using the 'wall pass', otherwise known as the quick one-two.

EXERCISE

In a non-pressurised situation, involving four players, A carries the ball forward towards a static defender (in this case a cone) and before reaching the defender, plays the ball to B before running around the opposite side to receive the one-touch return pass. A then delivers the ball safely to C who then repeats the exercise returning the ball to D, and in this way the exercise continues. Eventually a defender can be used to make the exercise more challenging, with all players being rotated every few minutes.

The exercise can progress into a five-a-side game, the diagram below shows how additional players (W) on the touchline can be used as 'walls' with just one touch available to help the man in possession of the ball.

Each touchline player can move up and down the touchline, but not enter the pitch - they can also play for either team.

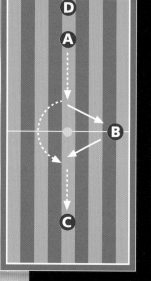

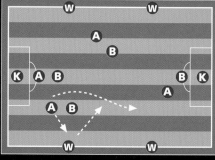

KEY FACTORS

1. **Look to commit the defender before passing - do not play the ball too early.**
2. **Pass the ball firmly and to feet.**
3. **Accelerate past defender after passing.**
4. **Receiver (B) make themselves available for the pass.**
5. **B delivers a return pass, weighted correctly, into space.**

If done correctly, this is a tactic which is extremely difficult to stop, but needs teamwork and communication between the two attacking players.

SOCCER SKILLS

CASPER
DE NORRE

A-Z

ARE YOU READY TO TACKLE OUR MILLWALL A-Z FOOTBALL QUIZ?

THE SIMPLE RULE IS THAT THE ANSWERS RUN THROUGH THE 26 LETTERS OF THE ALPHABET.

A

From which Premier League club have the Lions loaned full-back Brooke Norton-Cuffy for the 2023/24 season?

A

B

What nationality is summer signing Casper de Norre?

B

C

Which Millwall legend scored the goal that took The Lions to the 2004 FA Cup final?

C

D

Can you name the famous Millwall manager who led the club to the top-flight of English football for the first time in 1988?

D

E

Who scored The Lions' first Championship goal of the 2023/24 season?

E

F

Who is Millwall's current number 10?

F

G

Millwall's record League goalscorer and former manager **Neil Harris** is currently managing which League Two team?

G _____

K Which Lions' legend made a club record 523 League appearances for the club?

K _____

L Young Millwall defender Alex Mitchell is currently on loan at which League One club?

L _____

M **Millwall signed Duncan Watmore from which Championship rival?**

M _____

H Which member of The Lions' 2023/24 squad joined from Fulham the summer of 2016?

H _____

I Which of Millwall's 2023/24 Championship rivals play their home games at Portman Road?

I _____

J In which month of the year will Millwall begin their 2023/24 FA Cup campaign?

J _____

ANSWERS ON PAGE 62

Q

Who is providing Millwall's 2023 Boxing Day opposition at The Den?

Q

R

Which defender joined The Lions from Gillingham in 2015 and made over 200 first-team appearances for the club?

R

S

At which club did Lions' midfielder George Honeyman begin his career?

S

T

The Lions registered their record 9-1 League victory over which Devon-based club back in 1927?

T

N

Who scored his first Millwall goal to give The Lions a 1-0 Championship victory over Stoke City in August 2023?

N

O

Can you name the forward who progressed through the Millwall youth system and played in the first-team last season before joining Stockport County in January 2023?

O

P

What nationality is Lions' 'keeper Bartosz Białkowski?

P

W In which country will The Lions complete their final Championship game of the 2023/24 season?

W

X What is the christian name of the manager who will be in the opposing dugout when The Lions face Sheffield Wednesday in 2023/24?

X

U Can you name the midfielder who joined The Lions from Yeovil Town in the January 2014 transfer window?

U

Y From which club did The Lions sign central defender Byron Webster in the June 2014?

Y

V Can you name the Millwall forward who left The Den in the 2023 summer transfer window?

V

Z On which Road is The Den located?

Z

A-Z

PART TWO

ANSWERS ON PAGE 62

BILLY
MITCHELL

8

DESIGN A FOOTBALL BOOT

Design a brilliant new football boot for The Lions squad!

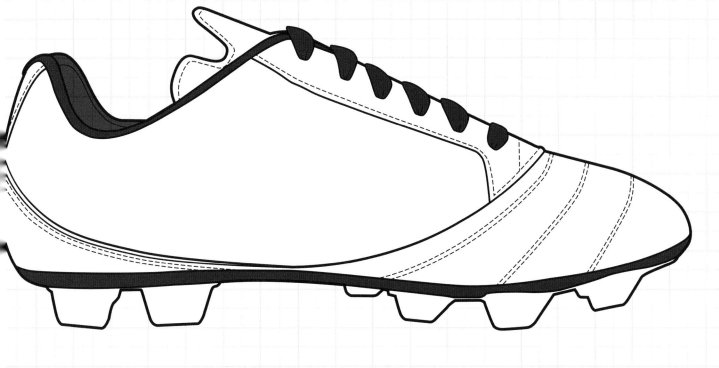

MIDFIELD
MAESTROS

ALEX RAE, TIM CAHILL AND NADJIM ABDOU WERE ALL REAL CREATORS IN THE LIONS MIDFIELD. CONTINUING THAT FINE MILLWALL TRADITION IS ACADEMY PRODUCT BILLY MITCHELL.

A man who needs little introduction, Tim Cahill arrived at The Den as a fresh-faced youngster in 1997 and left SE16 as a multi-million-pound Premier League player and international footballer in 2004.

With a knack of arriving late in the penalty area to score headers, the Australian quickly endeared himself to the Millwall faithful with a string of fine performances and goals.

Cahill scored perhaps the most famous goal in the history of Millwall Football Club, finding the net at Old Trafford in the 2004 FA Cup Semi-Final victory over Sunderland.

Tough-tackling and no-nonsense Scot, Alex Rae, became the bedrock of Millwall's team over the course of six seasons in the early-mid 90s.

Joining from Falkirk in 1990, Rae left for Sunderland in 1996 having played over 250 times for The Lions, scoring 71 goals.

Regularly at the top of the club's goalscoring charts season-upon-season, the Glaswegian is firmly entrenched in the hearts of Millwall fans.

ALEX RAE

DATE OF BIRTH:	30 September 1969
PLACE OF BIRTH:	Glasgow, Scotland
NATIONALITY:	Scottish
LIONS APPEARANCES:	258
LIONS GOALS:	71
LIONS DEBUT:	25 August 1990
	Watford 1-1 Millwall (Division Two)

TIM CAHILL

DATE OF BIRTH:	16 December 1979
PLACE OF BIRTH:	Sydney, Australia
NATIONALITY:	Australian
LIONS APPEARANCES:	260
LIONS GOALS:	57
LIONS DEBUT:	2 May 1998
	Millwall 1-2 AFC Bournemouth (Division Two)

Going through the generations of Millwall Football Club you will always find those who mean just that little bit more than anyone else to Lions supporters.

It's safe to say that Nadjim 'Jimmy' Abdou falls under that category.

Whether it's his effervescent performances, his man-marking of so-called superstars or scoring that crucial Play-Off Semi-Final goal at Elland Road against Leeds United in 2009, Abdou has rubber-stamped his lifetime passport to happiness in SE16.

JIMMY ABDOU

DATE OF BIRTH:	13 July 1984
PLACE OF BIRTH:	Martigues France
NATIONALITY:	French
LIONS APPEARANCES:	342
LIONS GOALS:	9
LIONS DEBUT:	9 August 2008

Oldham Athletic 4-3 Millwall (League One)

BILLY MITCHELL

DATE OF BIRTH:	22 April 2000
PLACE OF BIRTH:	London
NATIONALITY:	English
LIONS APPEARANCES:	111 *
LIONS GOALS:	1 *
LIONS DEBUT:	5 May 2019

Wigan Athletic 1-0 Millwall (Championship)

*AS AT THE END OF THE 2022/23 SEASON

Another product of Millwall's successful youth Academy, Billy Mitchell is now a mainstay in The Lions' first-team squad.

A debut on the final day of the 2018/19 campaign at Wigan Athletic kickstarted the midfielder's fledgling career, with his 100th game for the club coming in a 2-1 win at Queens Park Rangers in 2023.

Supporters will hope to see much more from Mitchell, who is moulding himself into a potential Millwall great already at such a young age.

CLASSIC
FAN'TASTIC

Zampa the Lion is hiding in the crowd in five different places as Millwall fans celebrate at Old Trafford during the FA Cup Semi-Final success in 2004.

Can you find all five?
ANSWERS ON PAGE 62

GEORGE SAVILLE

23

19

DUNCAN WATMORE

GOAL
OF THE SEASON

Zian Flemming's outstanding strike at Rotherham United bagged Millwall Football Club's 2022/23 Goal of the Season award.

With The Lions 1-0 behind at the AESSEAL New York Stadium on 5th October courtesy of an early penalty-kick from Dan Barlaser, Flemming picked up the ball three minutes from the half-time break and proceeded to take a touch before curling a stunning effort into the top corner from around 25 yards out.

Despite applying second-half pressure, The Lions had to make to do with just a point from Yorkshire, but the goal stuck in the memory of Millwall supporters enough to be voted into first place.

Many other candidates were in contention to take the crown - including a solo effort of Flemming's at Stoke City in February - but the goal against The Millers saw off all competition.

ZIAN FLEMMING

BEHIND THE

BADGE

...HIDDEN BEHIND OUR BEAUTIFUL BADGE?

A

B

C

D

F

G

E

H

ZIAN

FLEMMING

10

HAVE FUN COLOURING IN
THIS PICTURE OF LIONS STAR
ZIAN FLEMMING

TRUE
COLOURS

STUNNING STRIKERS

TEDDY SHERINGHAM, NEIL HARRIS AND STEVE MORISON WERE ALL ACE MARKSMEN FOR MILLWALL. LOOKING TO FOLLOW IN THEIR FOOTSTEPS IS TOM BRADSHAW.

Someone else who certainly needs no introduction to Lions supporters is Neil Harris.

Everything that could be said about this bona fide Millwall legend has already been mentioned, but over 13 seasons, the striker made himself one of the most popular players ever in SE16 with his 138 goals, which trumped Teddy Sheringham into making himself the all-time leading goalscorer in Millwall history.

Not content with that, Harris then returned as manager, steering The Lions to a League One Play-Off Final victory in 2017.

Millwall great Teddy Sheringham's storied career exploded into life at The 'old' Den, with his 111 goals comfortably sitting him as the club's all-time leading goalscorer - until Harris came along.

Sheringham scored 38 goals in one season in the early 90s and formed a formidable partnership with Tony Cascarino, one which would go down in Millwall folklore, before moving on to the likes of Manchester United - where he won the Champions League - and numerous England caps.

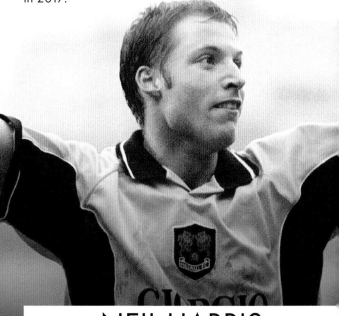

TEDDY SHERINGHAM

DATE OF BIRTH:	2 April 1966
PLACE OF BIRTH:	Highams Park
NATIONALITY:	English
LIONS APPEARANCES:	262
LIONS GOALS:	111
LIONS DEBUT:	15 January 1984
	Millwall 1-2 Brentford (Division Three)

NEIL HARRIS

DATE OF BIRTH:	12 July 1977
PLACE OF BIRTH:	Orsett
NATIONALITY:	English
LIONS APPEARANCES:	431
LIONS GOALS:	138
LIONS DEBUT:	4 April 1998
	Millwall 1-1 Bristol Rovers (Division Two)

Third on that Lions all-time leading goalscorers list is another SE16 legend Steve Morison.

In three spells at The Den, 'Moro' managed to find the net 92 times, winning two Play-Off Final trophies and one Player of the Year crown.

Morison stormed to the top of the goalscoring charts in his first two seasons at the club before moving to Norwich City and Leeds United, but he then returned to drive the club onto Wembley victory in 2017.

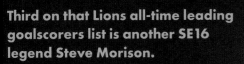

STEVE MORISON

DATE OF BIRTH:	29 August 1983
PLACE OF BIRTH:	Enfield
NATIONALITY:	English
LIONS APPEARANCES:	336
LIONS GOALS:	92
LIONS DEBUT:	8 August 2009

Southampton 1-1 Millwall (League One)

TOM BRADSHAW

DATE OF BIRTH:	27 July 1992
PLACE OF BIRTH:	Shrewsbury
NATIONALITY:	Welsh
LIONS APPEARANCES:	165*
LIONS GOALS:	41*
LIONS DEBUT:	26 August 2018

Rotherham United 1-0 Millwall (Championship)

*AS AT THE END OF THE 2022/23 SEASON

Currently spearheading The Lions' attack, Tom Bradshaw became - at the time - Millwall Football Club's record buy on his arrival at the club in 2018.

The Welshman enjoyed his best season to date in 2022/23 as he found the net 17 times, pushing Millwall to the cusp of the top six in the Sky Bet Championship, also earning international honours for the first time in five years.

At the time of writing, Bradshaw is hunting down both 200 appearances and 50 goals in a Millwall shirt.

REWIND

Millwall 3
Coventry City 2

SKY BET CHAMPIONSHIP · 13 AUGUST 2022

On a baking hot day in South London, The Lions showed fighting spirit to come from 2-0 down at home to Coventry City to win 3-2.

Early strikes from Kyle McFadzean and Matty Godden put The Sky Blues ahead before the half-hour, but Jake Cooper got Millwall back into things before the half-time break, before goals from George Honeyman - his first for the club - and George Saville (in the 85th minute) secured a priceless win for Gary Rowett's side.

Swansea City 2
Millwall 2

SKY BET CHAMPIONSHIP · 16 AUGUST 2022

Just three nights after that dramatic success over Coventry City, a even more incredible sequence of events took place in South Wales against Swansea City.

Ryan Manning's first-minute effort and Michael Obafemi's 12th-minute strike looked to have done enough for The Swans, but two own-goals deep into stoppage-time secured the most unlikely draw for The Lions - and who can forget Ryan Leonard's match-saving tackle at 2-1!

Blackpool 2
Millwall 3

SKY BET CHAMPIONSHIP · 28 APRIL 2023

A breathless Sky Bet Championship Friday night encounter at Bloomfield Road kept Millwall in the hunt for a place in the Play-Offs.

A back-and-forth match saw Tom Bradshaw put The Lions into a second-minute lead, before The Tangerines equalised through a dubious Jerry Yates penalty-kick, leaving the score level at the break. Bradshaw then scored again to make it 2-1, only for the hosts to peg Millwall back again with 67 minutes played. Zian Flemming, however, slotted home a penalty-kick 15 minutes from time to win the three points.

FAST FORWARD

Millwall
v Southampton

SKY BET CHAMPIONSHIP · 24 FEBRUARY 2024

With Southampton installed as one of the favourites for promotion from the Sky Bet Championship and an instant return to the Premier League, Russell Martin's side will provide a tough test for Millwall to finish the shortest month of the year.

However, The Lions tend to thrive against bigger opposition, meaning a blockbuster event is in store for all at The Den on 24th February.

Leeds United
v Millwall

SKY BET CHAMPIONSHIP · 16 MARCH 2024

There have been some memorable matches between Leeds United and Millwall over the years, with this encounter expected to be no different.

That 4-3 win at Elland Road will stick in the memories of Lions fans forever - and with Leeds recently relegated from a stint at English football's top table, there is expected to be a powder keg atmosphere as the two clubs lock horns in mid-March.

Swansea City
v Millwall

SKY BET CHAMPIONSHIP · 4 MAY 2024

Last season, Millwall Football Club's season ended with defeat at home to Blackburn Rovers on the final day.

This time around, Gary Rowett's side will visit Swansea City for their last game of the campaign. If qualification for top six is up for grabs, you can expect this day to weigh heavily on the minds of all concerned.

BEING
PREDICTABLE
IS EASY
IN FOOTBALL.

DOING THE
UNEXPECTED
IS A LOT MORE
DIFFICULT.

TURNING
WITH THE BALL

One of the biggest problems a defence can have to deal with is when a skilful player is prepared to turn with the ball and run at them, committing a key defender into making a challenge. Because football today is so fast and space so precious, this is becoming a rare skill.

EXERCISE 1

In an area 20m x 10m, A plays the ball into B who turns, and with two touches maximum plays the ball into C. C controls and reverses the process. After a few minutes the middleman is changed.

As you progress, a defender is brought in to oppose B, and is initially encouraged to play a 'passive' role. B has to turn and play the ball to C who is allowed to move along the baseline.

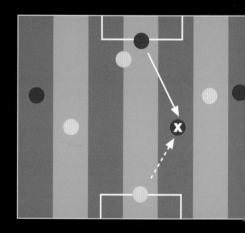

The type of turns can vary. Players should be encouraged to use the outside of the foot, inside of the foot, with feint and disguise to make space for the turn.

EXERCISE 2

As the players grow in confidence, you can move forward to a small-sided game. In this example of a 4-a-side practice match, X has made space for himself to turn with the ball, by coming off his defender at an angle. By doing this he can see that the defender has not tracked him, and therefore has the awareness to turn and attack.

Matches at the top level are won and lost by pieces of skill such as this, so players have to be brave enough to go in search of the ball, and turn in tight situations.

SOCCER SKILLS

MILLWALL FOOTBALL CLUB
1885

15

JOE
BRYAN

HIGH FIVES

HOW GOOD IS YOUR LIONS KNOWLEDGE?

PUT YOUR MEMORY TO THE TEST WITH OUR HIGH FIVES QUIZ

1. Across the previous five seasons, who have been Millwall's leading League goalscorers?

1. _____
2. _____
3. _____
4. _____
5. _____

3. Prior to Gary Rowett, who were the club's last five permanent managers?

1. _____
2. _____
3. _____
4. _____
5. _____

2. Can you name The Lions' last five FA Cup opponents ahead of the 2023/24 season?

1. _____
2. _____
3. _____
4. _____
5. _____

4. Can you name our last five EFL Cup opponents as at the end of the 2022/23 season?

1. _____
2. _____
3. _____
4. _____
5. _____

5. Can you remember Millwall's final League position from each of the last five seasons?

1.
2.
3.
4.
5.

8. Can you recall the score and season from our last five victories over rivals West Ham United?

1.
2.
3.
4.
5.

6. Which members of the Millwall squad started the most League fixtures last season?

1.
2.
3.
4.
5.

9. Can you remember The Lions' final five Championship victories from last season?

1.
2.
3.
4.
5.

7. Can you recall the following players' squad numbers from the 2022/23 season?

1. **Shaun Hutchinson**
2. **George Saville**
3. **Zian Flemming**
4. **Ryan Leonard**
5. **George Honeyman**

10. Can you recall the club's end of season points tally from the last five seasons?

1.
2.
3.
4.
5.

ANSWERS ON PAGE 62

Millwall Football Club — 1885

SENSATIONAL STOPPERS

KASEY KELLER, TONY WARNER AND DAVID FORDE WERE ALL GREAT LIONS 'KEEPERS. CONTINUING THAT PROUD TREND IS CURRENT STOPPER MATIJA ŠARKIĆ.

Nicknamed 'Denzil' due to his remarkable likeness for the 'Only Fools and Horses' character, Tony Warner was a part of the Millwall side which won the 2000/01 Division Two title at a canter, before playing his part in the push for promotion to the Premier League the following season.

"Denzil, Denzil, what's the score?" could often be heard ringing around The Den as The Lions notched up another hatful of strikes - with Warner always responding in kind.

Born in Washington, American Kasey Keller certified his status as a Millwall hero between the sticks across five seasons in SE16.

Signed on a free transfer from Portland University in 1992, the stopper then made just over 200 appearances in a Lions shirt, becoming the last goalkeeper to play at The 'old' Den and the first to play at The 'new' Den.

Keller left for Leicester City having been a part of famous FA Cup wins over Arsenal and Chelsea in 1995.

KASEY KELLER

DATE OF BIRTH:	27 November 1969
PLACE OF BIRTH:	Washington, USA
NATIONALITY:	American
LIONS APPEARANCES:	202
LIONS DEBUT:	2 May 1992

Millwall 2-0 Southend United (Division Two)

TONY WARNER

DATE OF BIRTH:	11 May 1974
PLACE OF BIRTH:	Liverpool
NATIONALITY:	English
LIONS APPEARANCES:	225
LIONS DEBUT:	7 August 1999

Cardiff City 1-1 Millwall (Division Two)

Irish goalkeeper David Forde played almost 350 times for Millwall Football Club, cementing himself as one of the club's greatest ever stoppers in his eight seasons with The Lions.

Signed from Cardiff City on a free transfer in 2008, 'Fordey' was a two-time Play-Off Finalist under Kenny Jackett's reign as manager, eventually winning promotion to The Championship at the second attempt in 2010 as The Lions defeated Swindon Town 1-0.

After staving off relegation back to League One in 2013/14, a now famous photo of Forde with late Chairman, John Berylson, and two cigars was born.

DAVID FORDE

DATE OF BIRTH: 20 December 1979

PLACE OF BIRTH: Galway, Ireland

NATIONALITY: Irish

LIONS APPEARANCES: 339

LIONS DEBUT: 9 August 2008
Oldham Athletic 4-3 Millwall (League One)

MATIJA ŠARKIĆ

DATE OF BIRTH: 23 July 1997

PLACE OF BIRTH: Grimsby

NATIONALITY: Montenegrin

LIONS APPEARANCES: 5*

LIONS DEBUT: 5 August 2023
Middlesbrough 0-1 Millwall (Championship)

*AS OF 2 SEPTEMBER 2023

Millwall Football Club announced the signing of Matija Šarkić from Wolverhampton Wanderers on 3 August 2023.

The 26-year-old goalkeeper joined the club on a long-term contract for an undisclosed fee and became number five in the door for Gary Rowett during the 2023 summer transfer window. Šarkić, born in Grimsby, is a Montenegro international and possessed Sky Bet Championship experience aplenty prior to his move to SE16.

The stopper made his Lions debut on the opening day of the 2023/24 season at Middlesbrough and will look to cement the number one spot in the years to come.

ANSWERS

PAGE 29: FOOTY PHRASES
Keepie Uppie.

PAGE 34: A-Z QUIZ
A. Arsenal. B. Belgian. C. Cahill, Tim. D. Doherty, John. E. Esse, Romain.
F. Flemming, Zian. G. Gillingham. H, Hutchinson, Shaun. I. Ipswich Town.
J. January. K. Kitchener, Barry. L. Lincoln City. M. Middlesbrough. N. Nisbet, Kevin.
O. Olaofe, Isaac. P. Polish. Q. Queens Park Rangers. R. Romeo, Mahlon.
S. Sunderland. T. Torquay United. U. Upson, Ed. V. Voglsammer, Andreas.
W. Wales (away to Swansea City). X. Xisco, Muñoz. Y. Yeovil Town. Z. Zampa Road.

PAGE 42: FAN'TASTIC

PAGE 48: BEHIND THE BADGE
A. Danny McNamara. B. Joe Bryan.
C. Casper De Norre. D. Kevin Nisbet.
E. George Saville. F. Billy Mitchell.
G. Duncan Watmore. H. Kevin Nisbet.

PAGE 58: HIGH FIVES

QUIZ 1:
1. 2022/23, Tom Bradshaw (17 goals).
2. 2021/22, Benik Afobe (12 goals).
3. 2020/21, Jed Wallace (11 goals).
4. 2019/20, Matt Smith (13 goals).
5. 2018/19, Lee Gregory (10 goals).

QUIZ 2:
1. 2022/23, Sheffield United (third round).
2. 2021/22, Crystal Palace (third round).
3. 2020/21, Bristol City (fourth round).
4. 2020/21, Boreham Wood (third round) .
5. 2019/20, Sheffield United (fourth round).

QUIZ 3:
1. Neil Harris. 2. Ian Holloway. 3. Steve Lomas.
4. Kenny Jackett. 5. Willie Donachie.

QUIZ 4:
1. Cambridge United (2022/23). 2. Leicester City (2021/22).
3. Cambridge United (2021/22). 4. Portsmouth (2021/22).
5. Burnley (2020/21).

QUIZ 5:
1. 8th in Championship (2022/23). 2. 9th in Championship (2021/22).
3. 11th in Championship (2020/21). 4. 8th in Championship (2019/20).
5. 21st in Championship (2018/19).

QUIZ 6:
1. Jake Cooper (45 Championship starts).
2. Zian Fleming & Dan McNamara (both made 40 Championship starts).
3. Tom Bradshaw (38 Championship starts).
4. Murray Wallace (37 Championship starts).
5. George Saville (36 Championship starts).

QUIZ 7:
1. 4. 2. 23. 3. 10. 4. 18. 5. 39.

QUIZ 8:
1. 2004/05, Millwall 1-0 West Ham United (Championship).
2. 2003/04, Millwall 4-1 West Ham United (Football League First Division).
3. 1992/93, Millwall 2-1 West Ham United (Football League First Division).
4. 1978/79, Millwall 2-1 West Ham United (Division Two)
5. 1932/33, Millwall 1-0 West Ham United 0 (Division Two)

QUIZ 9:
1. Blackpool 2-3 Millwall. 2. Millwall 2-0 Preston North End.
3. Millwall 2-1 Swansea City. 4. Reading 0-1 Millwall.
5. Stoke City 0-1 Millwall.

QUIZ 10:
1. 2022/23, 68 points. 2. 2021/22, 69 points. 3. 2020/21, 62 points.
4. 2019/20, 68 points. 5. 2018/19, 44 points.